COCKTAIL RECIPES 2022

FOR BEGINNERS

JUAN GUERRA

TABLE OF CONTENTS

MALIBU PINEAPPLETINI	12
MALIBU RUM-BALL	13
MALIBU SOL	14
MALIBU SUMMER RAIN	15
MALIBU SUNTAN	16
MALIBU SWEET SIN	17
MALIBU TEQUILA BANANA	18
MALIBU TROPICAL BANANA SEX-A-PEEL	19
MALIBU TROPICAL BREEZE	20
MALIBU TROPICAL EXPLOSION	21
MALIBU TROPICAL OASIS	22
MALIBU TROPICAL SANGRIA	23
MALIBU TROPICAL SOUR	24
MALIBU TROPICAL SUNRISE	25
MALIBU VANILLA BANANA-TINI	26
MALIBU VANILLA DREAM	27
MAMA WANA	28
MAMBO KING	29
MAN EATER	30
MANGO BAJITO	31
MANGO (OR GUAVA) DAIQUIRI	32
MANGO FROZEN DREAM	33
MANGO MADRAS	34
MANGO MAI TAI	35
MANGO MAMBO	36

MANGO SPARKLER	37
MARTI MOJO	38
MARY PICKFORD	39
MIAMI SPECIAL	40
MILLIONAIRE	41
THE MILLIONAIRE AND HIS WIFE	42
MISSION MADNESS	43
MO BAY MARTINI	44
MOJITO (267 SIGNATURE MANGO)	45
MOJITO (APPLE PEAR)	46
MOJITO (BEE)	47
MOJITO (BERMUDA GOLD)	48
MOJITO (BIG APPLE)	49
MOJITO (BRINLEY LIME)	50
MOJITO (COCO RUM)	51
MOJITO (CUCUMBER)	52
MOJITO (GINGER)	53
MOJITO (GRAND MELON)	54
MOJITO (LIMÓN RUM)	55
MOJITO (LOW CAL BACARDI)	56
MOJITO (MALIBU MANGO)	57
MOJITO (MALIBU PASSION FRUIT)	58
MOJITO (MILLIONAIRE)	59
MOJITO (MALIBU NOCHE BLANCA)	60
MOJITO (O)	61
MOJITO (ORIGINAL BACARDI)	62
MOJITO (PEACH RED RUM)	63

MOJITO (SONNY'S)	64
MOJITO (SPICY)	65
MOJITO (TRADITIONAL/CUBAN)	66
MOJITO (WATER CLUB)	67
MOJITO (WILD BERRY)	68
MOJITO (WINTER)	69
MOJITO MARTINI	70
MOM'S SANGRIA	71
MONKEY SPECIAL	72
MONKEY WRENCH	73
MONTEGO MARGARITA	74
MOONLIGHT SAIL	75
THE MORGAN CANNONBALL	76
MORGAN'S JOLLY ROGER	77
MORGAN'S RED ROUGE	78
MORGAN'S SPICED RUM ALEXANDER	79
MORGAN'S WENCH	80
THE MOUNT GAY GRINDER	81
MR. LICK	82
MTB & GINGER	83
MUFFLED SCREECH	84
MYERS'S APPLESAUCE	85
MYERS'S HEAT WAVE	86
MYERS'S HONEY POT	87
MYERS'S LEMON DROP	88
MYERS'S LOUNGE LIZARD	89
MYERS'S RUM AND TROPICAL HOT COCOA	90

MYERS'S RUM BARREL 91

MYERS'S RUM COZY 92

MYERS'S RUM HOLIDAY GROG 93

MYERS'S RUM HOLIDAY NOG 94

MYERS'S RUM PLANTER'S PUNCH 95

MYERS'S RUM SHARKBITE 96

MYERS'S RUM SUNSHINE COCKTAIL 97

MYERS'S SIZZLER 98

MYRTLE BANK PUNCH 99

NAVY GROG 100

NEON 101

NEWFOUNDLAND NIGHT-CAP 102

NILLA COLA 103

NINETINI 104

NUFF RUM 105

NYOTA (SWAHILI FOR STAR) 106

THE OLD BERMUDIAN 107

"ONE-GRAND" COCKTAIL 108

ORANGE BOWL 109

ORANGE COLADA 110

ORIGINAL PIÑA COLADA 111

ORO & SODA 112

ORO COSMO 113

ORO GIMLET 114

ORO ON THE ROCKS 115

THE OTHER WOMAN 116

GOSLING'S ORANGE CIDER MARTINI 117

GRAPE PUNCH	118
GRASSHOPPER	119
GRAVE DIGGER	120
GREAT WHITE	121
GREEN MONKEY	122
GREEN PARROT	123
GUAYAVITA	124
HAPPY ENDINGS' GILLIGAN	125
HARD HAT	126
HAVANA BANANA FIZZ	127
HAVANA SIDECAR	128
HAVANA SPECIAL	129
HAWAIIAN DAISY	130
HAWAIIAN HULA	131
HAWAIIAN NIGHT	132
HAWAIIAN PLANTATION COBBLER	133
HEMINGWAY DAIQUIRI	134
HOLY BANANA COW	135
HOT BUTTERED RUM	136
HOT RUM AND CIDER PUNCH	137
HOT VOODOO DADDY	138
HOURGLASS	139
HUMMER	140
HURRICANE ANDREW	141
ICE BREAKER	142
IN THE PINK	143
INDIFFERENT MISS	144

INTERNATIONAL MAI TAI	145
ISLA GRANDE ICED TEA	146
ISLAND SUNSET	147
ISLAND VOODOO	148
ITALIAN COLADA	149
JADE	150
JAMAICA SNOW	151
JAMAICAN HOLIDAY	152
JAMAICAN SHAKE	153
JAMAICAN SUNSET	154
JAMAICAN WAKE-UP CALL	155
JEALOUS LOVER	156
JONESTOWN COOL-AID	157
JUMBLE BREW	158
JUMP UP AND KISS ME	159
JUMP UP BANANA-NANA	160
JUNGLE FLAME	161
THE KAHLUA COLADA	162
KEY LIME DREAM	163
KEY WEST SONG	164
KILLA' COLA	165
KILLER COLADA	166
"KILLER" RITA	167
KINGSTON COFFEE	168
KINGSTON COSMO	169
KINGSTON SOUR	170
KOKO-COLA	171

KON-TIKI	172
LABADU	173
LADY HAMILTON	174
LAUGHTER	175
LIGHT 'N STORMY	176
LIME FIZZ	177
LIME LUAU	178
LIMÓN MERINGUE PIE SHOT DRINK	179
LOVE POTION	180
LOVE STICK	181
LUCKY LADY	182
MALIBU ACOMPÁÑAME	183
MALIBU AFTER TAN	184
MALIBU BANANA COW	185
MALIBU BANANA-BERRY SPLIT	186
MALIBU BANANA MANGO BREEZE	187
MALIBU BANANA PADDY	188
MALIBU BANANA SPLIT	189
MALIBU BANANA TROPIC-TINI	190
MALIBU BANANA ZINGER	191
MALIBU BEACH	192
MALIBU BLUE LAGOON	193
MALIBU CARIBENO	194
MALIBU COCO COLADA MARTINI	195
MALIBU COCO-COSMO	196
MALIBU COCO-LIBRE	197
MALIBU COCONUT CREAMSICLE	198

MALIBU COCONUT REFRESHER 199

MALIBU ENDLESS SUMMER.. 200

MALIBU FRENCH KICK 201

MALIBU ISLA VIRGEN 202

MALIBU MANGO BAY BREEZE 203

MALIBU MANGO KAMIKAZE 204

MALIBU MANGO-LIME MARTINI 205

MALIBU MANGO MAI TAI... 206

MALIBU MARGARITA.. 207

MALIBU MEGA-NUT 208

MALIBU MEXICANA MAMA 209

MALIBU MIDNIGHT BREEZE 210

MALIBU NOCHE LIBRE 211

MALIBU ON THE BEACH 212

MALIBU ORANGE COLADA 213

MALIBU ORANGE PASSION.. 214

MALIBU PASSION FRUIT COSMO 215

MALIBU PASSION FRUIT SAKE-TINI 216

MALIBU PASSION POPPER 217

MALIBU PASSION TEA 218

MALIBU PINEAPPLE COSMOPOLITAN 219

MALIBU PINEAPPLETINI

2 parts Malibu pineapple rum

½ part triple sec

dash lime juice

splash orange juice

orange slice for garnish

Shake with ice and strain into a martini glass. Garnish with an orange slice.

MALIBU RUM-BALL

2 parts Malibu coconut rum

2 parts melon liqueur or melon puree

MALIBU SOL

3 parts Malibu coconut rum

½ part amaretto

½ part pineapple

½ part fresh lemon juice

Serve over ice in a rocks glass.

MALIBU SUMMER RAIN

1 part Malibu coconut rum

1 part Stoli vodka

1 part fresh lime juice

2 parts club soda

lime slice for garnish

Serve over ice in a tall glass and garnish with lime slice.

MALIBU SUNTAN

1½ oz. Malibu rum

5 oz. ice tea

lemon squeeze

Serve over ice.

MALIBU SWEET SIN

1 part Malibu mango rum

splash lime juice

splash cranberry juice

splash Bacardi 151 rum

MALIBU TEQUILA BANANA

1 part Malibu Tropical banana rum

1 part Tezón Reposado tequila

splash lime juice

MALIBU TROPICAL BANANA SEX-A-PEEL

1 part Malibu Tropical banana rum

½ part Frangelico

½ part Irish cream

cherry for garnish

Shake and serve on the rocks. Garnish with cherry.

MALIBU TROPICAL BREEZE

1 part Malibu coconut rum

1 part cranberry juice

2 parts pineapple juice

pineapple wedge for garnish

Serve in a tall glass and garnish with a pineapple wedge.

MALIBU TROPICAL EXPLOSION

2 parts Malibu coconut rum

2 parts pineapple juice

1 part pomegranate juice

Serve over ice in a tall glass.

MALIBU TROPICAL OASIS

2 parts Malibu coconut rum

1 part amaretto

2 parts frozen vanilla yogurt

1 part orange juice

1 part pineapple juice

dash honey

Blend and serve as a frozen shake.

MALIBU TROPICAL SANGRIA

2 parts Malibu Tropical banana rum

2 parts red wine

1 part 7UP

1 part orange juice

fresh fruit for garnish

cherry for garnish

Garnish with fresh fruits and cherry.

MALIBU TROPICAL SOUR

1¼ parts Malibu Tropical banana rum

¾ part Hiram Walker sour apple

¾ part fresh sour mix

orange corkscrew for garnish

Shake and strain into a martini glass. Garnish with orange corkscrew.

MALIBU TROPICAL SUNRISE

1½ parts Malibu Tropical banana rum

1 part orange juice

1 part lemon-lime soda

cherry for garnish

Garnish with cherry.

MALIBU VANILLA BANANA-TINI

1½ parts Malibu Tropical banana rum

2½ parts Stoli Vanil vodka

splash amaretto

orange twist for garnish

Garnish with orange twist.

MALIBU VANILLA DREAM

1 part Malibu coconut rum

½ part Stoli Vanil vodka

½ part pineapple juice

MAMA WANA

1 oz. Cruzan orange rum

1 oz. Cruzan banana rum

Pour into a glass over chunky ice.

MAMBO KING

1 oz. Tommy Bahama White Sand rum

1 oz. coconut rum

½ oz. Tommy Bahama Golden Sun rum

½ oz. banana liqueur

3 oz. pineapple juice

pineapple spear for garnish

Shake in a pilsner glass with ice. Garnish with pineapple spear.

MAN EATER

1 oz. Whaler's Great White rum

4 oz. cola

½ oz. grenadine

cherry for garnish

Pour into a cocktail glass over ice. Garnish with cherry.

MANGO BAJITO

1 oz. Captain Morgan spiced rum

½ oz. triple sec

3 oz. mango juice

splash champagne

Blend well with crushed ice. Serve in a cocktail or frappé glass.

MANGO (OR GUAVA) DAIQUIRI

1½ oz. One Barrel rum

½ oz. fresh-squeezed lime juice

¼ oz. simple syrup

¾ oz. mango nectar (or guava nectar)

1 tsp. sugar

lime wedge for garnish

Shake with ice and strain into a chilled martini glass. Garnish with lime wedge.

MANGO FROZEN DREAM

1¼ oz. Captain Morgan Parrot Bay mango rum

½ oz. amaretto

½ oz. triple sec

2 oz. orange juice

1 scoop vanilla ice cream

orange wheel for garnish

Blend until smooth with 1 cup ice and pour into a glass. Garnish with orange wheel.

MANGO MADRAS

1½ oz. Parrot Bay mango rum

2 oz. cranberry juice

2 oz. orange juice

orange wedge for garnish

Pour into a glass over ice and stir. Garnish with orange wedge.

MANGO MAI TAI

1¼oz. Captain Morgan Parrot Bay mango rum

1½ oz. margarita mix

1½ oz. pineapple juice

¼ oz. orgeat syrup

¼ oz. grenadine

pineapple slice for garnish

stemmed cherry for garnish

Shake with ice and pour into a glass. Garnish with pineapple slice and stemmed cherry.

MANGO MAMBO

1½ oz. Hiram Walker mango schnapps

1½ oz. Malibu Tropical banana rum

Shake with ice. Serve straight up in a chilled martini glass.

MANGO SPARKLER

¾ oz. One Barrel rum

¾ oz. mango nectar

2 oz. Moët nectar champagne

Stir with ice and strain into a chilled champagne flute.

MARTI MOJO

1 part Marti Autentico rum

1 part pineapple juice

1 part cranberry juice

mint sprig for garnish

pineapple for garnish

Shake well and serve in a martini glass. Garnish with fresh mint sprig and pineapple.

MARY PICKFORD

1½ oz. Puerto Rican white rum

1½ oz. pineapple juice

splash grenadine

Shake with 1 scoop crushed ice.

MIAMI SPECIAL

1 oz. Bacardi light rum

¼ oz. Hiram Walker white créme de menthe

¾ oz. lemon juice or Rose's lime juice

Shake and pour into a chilled martini glass.

MILLIONAIRE

¾ oz. Captain Morgan Original spiced rum

½ oz. créme de banana liqueur

2 oz. orange juice

1 oz. sour mix

½ oz. bar syrup

½ oz. grenadine

Blend first five ingredients with 1 cup crushed ice until slushy. Add grenadine and stir slightly.

THE MILLIONAIRE AND HIS WIFE

1 oz. Malibu mango rum

1 oz. Alize Red Passion liqueur

champagne

lemon twist for garnish

Shake first two ingredients with ice and strain into a martini glass. Top with champagne and garnish with a twist of lemon.

MISSION MADNESS

2 oz. Whaler's Vanille rum

¾ oz. amaretto

2 oz. passion fruit juice

2 oz. orange juice

lime slice for garnish

cherry for garnish

Fill hurricane glass with ice. Add ingredients into cocktail shaker and mix well. Pour over ice and garnish with lime slice and cherry.

MO BAY MARTINI

2 oz. Appleton Estate V/X Jamaica rum

¼ oz. extra dry vermouth

olive for garnish

Shake with ice and strain into a martini glass. Garnish with olive.

MOJITO (267 SIGNATURE MANGO)

2½ oz. 267 Infusion mango rum

4 fresh mint sprigs (plus more for garnish)

splash soda water

lime wedge for garnish

Muddle four fresh mint sprigs at the bottom of a glass. Add Infusion mango rum with a splash of soda water. Garnish with lime wedge and more mint sprigs.

MOJITO (APPLE PEAR)

1 part Bacardi Limón

1 part Bacardi Big Apple

2 mint leaves

2 parts pineapple juice

2 parts club soda

2 lime wedges

1 tbsp. sugar

Mix sugar, mint leaves, and lime in a glass and crush well. Add Bacardi Limón, Bacardi Big Apple, and pineapple juice, then top off with club soda.

MOJITO (BEE)

1 part Bacardi Rum

3 parts club soda

12 mint leaves

juice of ½ lime

1 tbsp. honey

mint sprigs or lime wheel for garnish

Place mint leaves and crushed ice in a glass. Muddle well with a pestle. Add lime juice, honey, and Bacardi; stir well. Top off with club soda, stir, and garnish with sprigs of mint or a lime wheel.

MOJITO (BERMUDA GOLD)

2 oz. Gosling's Gold Bermuda rum

6–8 spearmint leaves

¼ oz. fresh lime juice

1 tsp. superfine sugar

½ oz. club soda

¼ oz. Gosling's Black Seal rum

In a large old-fashioned glass, muddle the lime juice, sugar, and spearmint leaves (save a couple for garnish), bruising the spearmint well. Add Gosling's Gold Bermuda rum and ice. Top with a splash of club soda and a float of Gosling's Black Seal rum. Garnish with remaining spearmint leaves.

MOJITO (BIG APPLE)

1 part Bacardi Big Apple rum

3 parts club soda

12 mint leaves

½ lime

½ part sugar

mint sprigs, lime wheel, or green apple slices for garnish

Place mint leaves, sugar, and lime in a glass. Crush well with a pestle. Add Bacardi Big Apple rum, top off with club soda, stir well, and garnish with sprigs of mint and a lime wheel or green apple slice.

MOJITO (BRINLEY LIME)

2 parts Brinley Gold lime rum

3 parts club soda

½ lime

6 mint leaves

1 tsp. sugar

Squeeze in and muddle ½ lime. Blend with crushed ice.

MOJITO (COCO RUM)

1 part Bacardi Coco rum

3 parts lemon-lime soda

12 mint leaves

½ lime

mint sprigs for garnish

Place mint leaves and lime in glass and crush well. Add rum and soda and garnish with sprigs of mint.

MOJITO (CUCUMBER)

1½ oz. 10 Cane rum

1 oz. fresh-squeezed lime juice

1 oz. simple syrup

8–10 mint leaves

4 pieces peeled cucumber

club soda to top

cucumber slice/stick for garnish

Place simple syrup, mint leaves, and cucumber in the bottom of a tall glass. Press gently with a muddler. Fill with cracked ice. Add 10 Cane and lime juice. Stir gently and top off with soda. Garnish with a slice or stick of cucumber.

MOJITO (GINGER)

1 part Bacardi rum

3 parts ginger beer

12 mint leaves

½ lime

½ part simple sugar

Same as Original Bacardi Mojito, but using ginger beer rather than club soda.

MOJITO (GRAND MELON)

1 part Bacardi Grand Melon rum

3 parts club soda

12 mint leaves

½ lime

½ part sugar

mint sprigs for garnish

lime wheel or watermelon slice for garnish

Place mint leaves, sugar, and lime in a glass. Crush well with a pestle. Add Bacardi Grand Melon rum, top off with club soda, stir well, and garnish with sprigs of mint and a lime wheel or watermelon slice.

MOJITO (LIMÓN RUM)

1 part Bacardi Limón rum

3 parts club soda

12 mint leaves

½ lime

½ part sugar

mint sprigs for garnish

lime or lemon wheel for garnish

Place mint leaves, sugar, and lime in a glass. Crush well with a pestle. Add Bacardi Limón rum, top off with club soda, stir well and garnish with sprigs of mint and a lime or lemon wheel.

MOJITO (LOW CAL BACARDI)

1 part Bacardi rum

3 parts club soda

12 mint leaves

½ lime

3 packets Splenda

mint sprigs for garnish

lime wedge for garnish

Place mint leaves, Splenda, and lime in glass. Muddle with pestle. Add Bacardi, then club soda. Stir well and garnish with mint sprigs and a lime wedge.

MOJITO (MALIBU MANGO)

2½ parts Malibu mango rum

½ part fresh lime juice

½ part simple syrup

3–4 mint sprigs (plus extra for garnish)

3 lime wedges (plus 1 for garnish)

2–3 splashes club soda

Pour lime juice and simple syrup into a glass. Add mint sprigs and lime wedges, and muddle contents thoroughly. Add ice, Malibu mango rum, and splashes of club soda. Garnish with a lime wedge and mint sprigs.

MOJITO (MALIBU PASSION FRUIT)

2 parts Malibu passion fruit rum

3 tbsp. fresh lemon juice

2 tbsp. sugar

club soda

fresh mint

MOJITO (MILLIONAIRE)

1½ oz. 10 Cane rum

½ oz. simple syrup

1 oz. fresh-squeezed lime juice

8–10 mint leaves

splash Moët & Chandon champagne

mint sprig for garnish

Place simple syrup and mint leaves in the bottom of a tall glass. Press gently with a muddler. Fill with cracked ice. Add 10 Cane and lime juice. Stir gently and top off with Moët & Chandon champagne. Garnish with a mint sprig.

MOJITO (MALIBU NOCHE BLANCA)

3 parts Malibu coconut rum

1 part fresh lime juice

1 part simple syrup

1 part club soda

8 mint leaves

lime wheel for garnish

Serve in a Collins glass. Garnish with a lime wheel.

MOJITO (O)

1 part Bacardi O rum

3 parts club soda

12 mint leaves

½ lime

½ part sugar

mint sprigs for garnish

lime or orange wheel for garnish

Place mint leaves, sugar, and lime in a glass. Muddle well with a pestle. Add Bacardi O rum, top off with club soda, stir well, and garnish with sprigs of mint and a lime or orange wheel.

MOJITO (ORIGINAL BACARDI)

1 part Bacardi rum

3 parts club soda

12 mint leaves

½ lime

½ part sugar

mint sprigs or lime wheel for garnish

Place mint leaves, sugar, and lime in a glass. Muddle well with a pestle. Add Bacardi, top off with club soda, stir well, and garnish with sprigs of mint or a lime wheel.

MOJITO (PEACH RED RUM)

1 part Bacardi Peach Red rum

3 parts club soda

12 mint leaves

½ peach

½ part sugar

mint sprigs for garnish

peach slice for garnish

Place mint leaves, sugar, and peach in a glass. Crush well with a pestle. Add Bacardi Peach Red rum, top off with club soda, stir well, and garnish with sprigs of mint and a peach slice.

MOJITO (SONNY'S)

½ lime, cut into wedges

2 tbsp. sugar

½ oz. Chateaux peppermint schnapps

1 oz. Bacardi Superior rum

ice

club soda to top

lime wheel for garnish

Muddle lime and sugar in the bottom of an 8-oz. glass. Add schnapps, ice, and Bacardi. Top with club soda and garnish with lime wheel.

MOJITO (SPICY)

1½ oz. Flor de Cana 4-year-old extra-dry rum

2 1-inch cubes watermelon

1 slice jalapeño

10 fresh mint leaves

¾ oz. fresh lime juice

½ oz. simple syrup

1½ oz. club soda

watermelon triangle for garnish

jalapeño slice for garnish

mint sprig for garnish

In a mixing glass, add jalapeno slice followed by watermelon cubes. Muddle with mint. Add Flor de Cana 4-year-old extra-dry rum, simple syrup, and lime juice. Add ice and shake. Strain over fresh ice into a highball glass and top with club soda. Integrate club soda with bar spoon. Garnish with watermelon triangle, slice of jalapeño, and mint sprig.

MOJITO
(TRADITIONAL/CUBAN)

1 oz. Bacardi light rum

1 tbsp. sugar

1 tbsp. lime juice

6-inch sprig of mint

ice to fill

3 oz. club soda

2 dashes Angostura bitters

Place sugar, lime juice, and mint in a Collins glass. Crush mint stalk with pestle and muddle with juice and sugar. Add rum, add ice to top of glass, and top off with club soda and bitters. Stir well. Enjoy!

MOJITO (WATER CLUB)

1½ oz. Bacardi light rum

½ oz. fresh-squeezed lemon juice

½ oz. fresh-squeezed lime juice

1 oz. Guarapo (sugar cane extract)

½ oz. blue curacao

6 mint leaves

splash club soda

fresh mint for garnish

Shake well with ice. Serve in a Collins glass and garnish with fresh mint.

MOJITO (WILD BERRY)

1½ oz. Pyrat XO Reserve rum

2–3 each fresh blackberries, blueberries, and raspberries

12–14 fresh mint leaves

juice of 1 lime

1 oz. simple syrup

spritz soda water

mint sprig for garnish

powdered sugar for garnish

Muddle mint, simple syrup, wild berries, and lime juice in a 14-oz. highball glass. Fill glass with crushed ice, then add Pyrat XO Reserve rum. Stir well until the ice is reduced by 1/3, then top with more crushed ice, stirring until glass begins to frost on the outside. Spritz with soda water and stir one last time to incorporate. Garnish with two long straws and a mint sprig that has been dusted with powdered sugar.

MOJITO (WINTER)

1½ oz. Ron Anejo Pampero Especial rum

¾ oz. fresh lemon juice

¼ oz. maple syrup

2 dashes Angostura bitters

6 sprigs mint

Muddle 5 mint sprigs and bitters in a shaker. Add Ron Anejo Pampero Especial rum, lime, and maple syrup. Let sit for 1 minute. Shake hard. Strain into a double old-fashioned glass over fresh ice. Garnish with remaining mint sprig. If made with hot water, it becomes a toddy.

MOJITO MARTINI

1½ oz. Bacardi Limón

½ oz. lemon vodka

½ lime, quartered

8 mint leaves

Fill martini glass with crushed ice to chill. Fill a shaker half full with crushed ice. Add the rest of the ingredients, cover, and shake for about 1 minute. Remove ice from glass and pour in the mojito.

MOM'S SANGRIA

8 Red Delicious apple slices

2 small oranges cut into thin quarters

12 strawberries, sliced

2 lemons cut in thin slices

12 oz. freshly squeezed orange juice

12 oz. fresh lemon juice

6 oz. simple syrup

2 cinnamon sticks

8 oz. Pyrat XO Reserve rum

8 oz. Citronge

2 bottles of Spanish red wine

7UP to top

Place above ingredients, excluding 7UP, into a large glass container. Cover and refrigerate overnight. When ready to serve, pour into a pitcher over ice, filling 2/3 of the way. Add fresh sliced fruits and top with 7UP. Stir gently to mix. Serve in wine glasses over ice.

MONKEY SPECIAL

1 oz. dark rum

1 oz. light rum

½ oz. banana, peeled

2 oz. vanilla/chocolate ice cream

shaved chocolate for garnish

Sprinkle with shaved chocolate.

MONKEY WRENCH

1½ oz. Sailor Jerry Spiced Navy rum

grapefruit juice to fill

Pour Sailor Jerry Spiced Navy rum over ice in a Collins glass. Fill with grapefruit juice and stir.

MONTEGO MARGARITA

1½ oz. Appleton Estate V/X rum

½ oz. triple sec

2 oz. lemon or lime juice

1 scoop crushed ice

Blend. Serve in a tall glass.

MOONLIGHT SAIL

1 oz. Admiral Nelson's raspberry rum

1 oz. Admiral Nelson's coconut rum

1 oz. vodka

1 oz. Arrow sloe gin

½ oz. amaretto

2 oz. orange juice

3 oz. pineapple juice

cherry for garnish

lemon twist for garnish

Shake well and pour into a tall glass over ice. Garnish with cherry and lemon twist.

THE MORGAN CANNONBALL

1¼ oz. Captain Morgan Original Spiced rum

3 oz. pineapple juice

white crème de menthe to float

Blend first two ingredients with ice. Float white crème de menthe. Serve in a tall glass.

MORGAN'S JOLLY ROGER

¾ oz. Captain Morgan Original spiced rum

¾ oz. cinnamon schnapps

Serve as a shot.

MORGAN'S RED ROUGE

1 oz. Captain Morgan Original spiced rum

½ oz. blackberry brandy

2 oz. pineapple juice

½ oz. lemon juice

Stir.

MORGAN'S SPICED RUM ALEXANDER

1 oz. Captain Morgan Original spiced rum

½ oz. créme de cacao

1 oz. heavy cream

grated nutmeg for dusting

Shake and strain into a glass. Dust with nutmeg.

MORGAN'S WENCH

¾ oz. Captain Morgan Original spiced rum

¾ oz. amaretto

dark crème de cacao to float

Serve as a shot.

THE MOUNT GAY GRINDER

1½ oz. Mount Gay rum

cranberry juice to fill

splash 7UP

Serve in a tall glass.

MR. LICK

1 oz. Gosling's Black Seal rum

1 oz. apricot liqueur

pineapple juice to fill

splash grenadine

Shake over ice and serve on the rocks.

MTB & GINGER

1½ parts Malibu Tropical banana rum

ginger ale

lemon slice for garnish

Garnish with lemon slice.

MUFFLED SCREECH

1 oz. Newfoundland Screech rum

¼ oz. triple sec or Grand Marnier

2 oz. cream or milk

Layer Newfoundland Screech and triple sec or Grand Marnier over a few ice cubes in a glass. Top with cream or milk. No one can hear you scream ...

MYERS'S APPLESAUCE

1½ shot Myers's rum

1 orange slice

6 oz. hot cider

Stir in a heat-proof mug.

MYERS'S HEAT WAVE

¾ oz. Myers's Original dark rum

½ oz. peach schnapps

6 oz. pineapple juice

1 splash grenadine

Pour first two ingredients into a glass over ice. Fill with juice and top with grenadine.

MYERS'S HONEY POT

2 oz. Myers's rum

1 tbsp. honey

6 oz. hot water

pinch grated nutmeg

In the bottom of a heat-proof mug, stir honey and Myers's rum until honey is dissolved. Fill with hot water. Stir until blended. Sprinkle with nutmeg. If desired, molasses can be substituted for honey.

MYERS'S LEMON DROP

1 shot Myers's rum

2–3 lumps sugar

juice of ½ lemon

6 oz. hot water

1 cinnamon stick

In a heat-proof mug, muddle sugar, Myers's rum, and lemon juice until sugar is dissolved. Add hot water. Stir with a cinnamon stick until well blended.

MYERS'S LOUNGE LIZARD

1 oz. Myers's rum

½ oz. Leroux amaretto

cola to fill

lime wedge for garnish

Mix first two ingredients in a tall glass over ice. Fill with cola. Garnish with lime wedge.

MYERS'S RUM AND TROPICAL HOT COCOA

16 oz. Myers's rum

4 oz. bittersweet hot chocolate

chocolate-covered strawberry for garnish

Pour into a mug and top with shaved bittersweet chocolate curls. Garnish with chocolate-covered strawberry.

MYERS'S RUM BARREL

1 shot Myers's rum

8 oz. hot cola-flavored beverage

lemon slice for garnish

Gently stir in a heat-proof glass or mug. Garnish with lemon slice.

MYERS'S RUM COZY

2 oz. Myers's rum

1 tsp. sugar

6 oz. hot tea

½ oz. triple sec

dash nutmeg

Stir first four ingredients in a heat-proof mug. Sprinkle with nutmeg.

MYERS'S RUM HOLIDAY GROG

1 oz. Myers's rum

4 oz. fresh apple cider, hot

thinly-sliced lemon and orange wheels studded with cloves for garnish

Pour into a mug. Garnish with lemon and orange wheels.

MYERS'S RUM HOLIDAY NOG

4 oz. Myers's rum

1 pint melted low-fat vanilla ice cream

maraschino cherries for garnish

mint sprigs for garnish

Mix in a large bowl and chill. Pour into champagne flutes and garnish each with a maraschino cherry and a fresh mint sprig. Serves 6 to 8.

MYERS'S RUM PLANTER'S PUNCH

1¼ oz. Myers's rum

3 oz. orange juice

juice of ? lemon or lime

1 tsp. superfine sugar

dash grenadine

orange slice for garnish

maraschino cherry for garnish

Shake or blend until frothy. Serve over shaved ice in a highball glass. Garnish with orange slice and maraschino cherry.

MYERS'S RUM SHARKBITE

1¼ oz. Myers's rum

orange juice to fill

splash Rose's grenadine

Pour Myers's rum into a tumbler over ice cubes. Fill with orange juice and add a splash of Rose's grenadine.

MYERS'S RUM SUNSHINE COCKTAIL

1¼ oz. Myers's rum

2 oz. orange juice

2 oz. grapefruit juice

½ tsp. superfine sugar

dash Angostura bitters

cherry for garnish

Shake with ice until frothy and strain into a highball glass over shaved ice. Garnish with cherry.

MYERS'S SIZZLER

1 shot Myers's rum

1 tbsp. powdered cocoa

1 tbsp. sugar

1 cup scalded milk

sweetened whipped cream to top

instant coffee or powdered cocoa for sprinkling

In a heat-proof mug, stir cocoa and sugar. Add hot milk and Myers's rum. Stir until cocoa is dissolved. Top with whipped cream and sprinkle with instant coffee or cocoa.

MYRTLE BANK PUNCH

1¼ oz. Captain Morgan Original spiced rum

¼ oz. grenadine

1 oz. lime juice

1 tsp. sugar

¼ oz. cherry liqueur

cherry for garnish

orange wedge for garnish

Pour first four ingredients into a 10-oz. glass over crushed ice. Top with cherry liqueur and garnish with cherry and orange wedge.

NAVY GROG

½ oz. Sailor Jerry Spiced Navy rum

½ oz. vodka

½ oz. tequila

½ oz. triple sec

1 oz. amaretto

1 oz. orange juice

1 oz. pineapple juice

1 oz. cranberry juice

orange slice for garnish

cherry for garnish

Mix with ice and pour into a hurricane glass. Garnish with orange slice and cherry.

NEON

5 oz. Captain Morgan Parrot Bay coconut rum

1 oz. Black Haus blackberry schnapps

3 oz. pineapple juice

Serve over ice.

NEWFOUNDLAND NIGHT-CAP

1¼ oz. Newfoundland Screech rum

1–2 tsp. brown sugar

coffee to fill

whipped cream to top

Pour first two ingredients into a coffee cup. Fill with coffee and stir. Top with whipped cream. Take this one to bed with you!

NILLA COLA

1 oz. Whaler's Vanille rum

5 oz. cola

lime squeeze

lime wedge for garnish

Pour into a cocktail glass over ice. Garnish with lime wedge.

NINETINI

1 oz. Angostura 1919 Premium rum

½ oz. orange curacao

2 oz. sweet and sour mix

½ tsp. sugar

4 dashes Angostura aromatic bitters

Shake.

NUFF RUM

2 oz. Wray & Nephew rum

3 oz. Stones ginger wine

½ oz. Limoncello

½ oz. peach syrup

3 dashes Angostura bitters

fresh apple juice to float

orange peel for garnish

lemon peel for garnish

Build in an old-fashioned glass over cubed ice and stir. Garnish with orange and lemon peel.

NYOTA (SWAHILI FOR STAR)

3 oz. Starr African rum

1½ oz. acerola puree

Llopart Rosa Cava champagne

yellow cherry for garnish

Shake first two ingredients with ice and strain into a martini glass. Top off with Llopart Rosa Cava or other champagne. Garnish with yellow cherry.

THE OLD BERMUDIAN

1½ oz. Gosling's Gold Bermuda rum

6 mint leaves

2 dashes bitters

½ oz. lime juice

½ oz. simple syrup

¼ oz. champagne

lime twist for garnish

Muddle mint leaves in a shaker half filled with ice. Add Gosling's rum, bitters, lime juice, and simple syrup. Shake well and pour into a Collins glass. Top with champagne. Garnish with lime twist.

"ONE-GRAND" COCKTAIL

1½ oz. One Barrel rum

½ oz. Grand Marnier

½ oz. mango nectar

¼ oz. fresh-squeezed lime juice

mango slice for garnish

Shake with ice and strain into a chilled martini glass. Garnish with a mango slice.

ORANGE BOWL

1 oz. Bacardi O rum

4 oz. orange juice

2 oz. ginger ale

1 oz. Bacardi Select rum

orange slice for garnish

cinnamon stick for garnish

Pour first four ingredients into a wine glass. Float Bacardi Select rum on top. Garnish with orange slice and cinnamon stick.

ORANGE COLADA

2 oz. Cruzan orange rum

1 15-oz. can Coco Lopez real cream of coconut

4 oz. pineapple juice

4 oz. orange juice

Blend with 4 cups of ice.

ORIGINAL PIÑA COLADA

2 oz. Puerto Rican light rum (or, for a different twist, try Captain Morgan Parrot Bay coconut rum)

1 oz. Coco Lopez real cream of coconut

1 oz. heavy cream

6 oz. fresh pineapple juice

pineapple wedge for garnish

maraschino cherry for garnish

Blend for 15 seconds with ½ cup crushed ice. Pour into a 12-oz. glass. Garnish with pineapple wedge and maraschino cherry. Add a red straw. Tip: For the best tropical taste, always use fresh pineapple juice, never canned or mixes.

ORO & SODA

2 oz. Oronoco rum

splash soda

lime wedge for garnish

Pour Oronoco rum into a rocks glass over ice. Splash with soda and stir. Garnish with lime wedge.

ORO COSMO

2 oz. Oronoco rum

1 tbsp. Grand Marnier

1 tbsp. cranberry juice

1 tbsp. lime juice

lime twist for garnish

Shake over ice and strain into a chilled martini glass. Garnish with lime twist.

ORO GIMLET

2 oz. Oronoco rum

2 wedges lime

2 oz. lime juice

splash tonic

splash soda

dash simple syrup

lime wedge for garnish

Muddle lime wedges in a shaker. Add Oronoco rum, lime juice, and simple syrup, and shake vigorously with crushed ice. Strain into a Collins glass over ice cubes. Top with equal splashes tonic and soda. Garnish with lime wedge.

ORO ON THE ROCKS

2 oz. Oronoco rum

lime slice for garnish

Pour Oronoco into a short rocks glass over ice cubes. Garnish with a freshly cut lime slice.

THE OTHER WOMAN

1 oz. Admiral Nelson's Premium vanilla rum

1 oz. white soda

splash cola

cherry for garnish

Pour into a cocktail glass and garnish with cherry.

GOSLING'S ORANGE CIDER MARTINI

3 oz. Gosling's Gold Bermuda rum

1 tsp. cinnamon-sugar mix

orange wedge

3 oz. mulled cider, chilled

¼ oz. orange juice

¼ oz. Cointreau

orange twist for garnish

Place cinnamon-sugar in a dish. Rub orange wedge around the rim of a martini glass and dip rim into cinnamon-sugar. Shake remaining ingredients over ice and strain into rimmed martini glass. Garnish with an orange twist.

GRAPE PUNCH

1¼ oz. Bacardi light rum

grape juice to fill

lime or lemon wedge

    Pour Bacardi light rum into a tall glass over ice. Fill with grape juice and add a squeeze of lime or lemon.

GRASSHOPPER

1 oz. Bacardi light rum

¼ oz. Hiram Walker green créme de menthe

½ oz. cream

    Blend with crushed ice.

GRAVE DIGGER

½ oz. Stroh 80 rum

½ oz. Malibu rum

½ oz. Midori

3 oz. pineapple juice

Serve over ice in a tall glass.

GREAT WHITE

1 oz. Whaler's Great White rum

1 oz. cranberry juice

4 oz. orange juice

lemon wedge for garnish

Pour ingredients into a cocktail glass over ice. Garnish with a lemon wedge.

GREEN MONKEY

1½ oz. Malibu Tropical banana rum

¾ part melon liquor

1½ oz. fresh sour

1½ oz. pineapple juice

Shake with ice. Serve over ice.

GREEN PARROT

1½ oz. Appleton Estate V/X rum

4 oz. orange juice

1 oz. blue curacao

orange slice for garnish

Pour ingredients, one at a time in the order listed above, into a large stemmed glass over ice. Do not mix. Garnish with an orange slice.

GUAYAVITA

1½ oz. Flor de Caña Grand Reserve 7-year-old rum

1 oz. guava pulp

2 oz. sour mix

Shake and serve on the rocks.

HAPPY ENDINGS' GILLIGAN

1 oz. Malibu coconut rum

1 oz. Malibu mango rum

1 oz. Malibu tropical banana rum

½ oz. cranberry juice

½ oz. pineapple juice

cherry for garnish

Shake with ice and serve on the rocks. Garnish with cherry.

HARD HAT

1¼ oz. Bacardi Silver rum

1¼ oz. fresh lime juice

1 tsp. sugar

¼ oz. Rose's grenadine

club soda to fill

Shake first three ingredients with ice and strain into a 10-oz. glass. Fill with club soda.

HAVANA BANANA FIZZ

2 oz. light rum

2½ oz. pineapple juice

1½ oz. fresh lime juice

3–5 dashes Peychaud's bitters

1/3 banana, sliced

bitter lemon soda to fill

Blend first five ingredients. Fill with bitter lemon soda.

HAVANA SIDECAR

1½ oz. Puerto Rican golden rum

¾ oz. lemon juice

¾ oz. triple sec

Mix with 3-4 ice cubes.

HAVANA SPECIAL

2 oz. white rum

1 tbsp. maraschino cherry liqueur

½ tbsp. sugar

1 oz. lemon or lime juice

Shake and serve on the rocks.

HAWAIIAN DAISY

1½ oz. Bacardi light rum

1 oz. pineapple juice

¼ oz. lemon or lime juice

¼ oz. grenadine

club soda to top

Pour first four ingredients into a glass and top with club soda.

HAWAIIAN HULA

1½ parts Malibu Tropical banana rum

¾ part guava nectar

¾ part fresh sour mix

orange corkscrew for garnish

    Shake and strain into a martini glass. Garnish with orange corkscrew.

HAWAIIAN NIGHT

1 oz. Bacardi light rum

¼ oz. Hiram Walker cherry-flavored brandy

pineapple juice to fill

Pour Bacardi light rum into a tall glass half filled with ice. Fill with pineapple juice and float cherry-flavored brandy on top.

HAWAIIAN PLANTATION COBBLER

1½ oz. Pyrat XO Reserve rum

½ oz. Citronge liqueur

1½ oz. fresh sweet and sour

½ oz. simple syrup

½ slice of peeled pineapple

ginger ale

mint sprig for garnish

crystallized ginger for garnish

    Shake first five ingredients. Fill with ginger ale, then pour into a glass over ice. Garnish with fresh mint sprig and crystallized ginger.

118

HEMINGWAY DAIQUIRI

1½ oz. 10 Cane rum

½ oz. Luxardo maraschino cherry liqueur

1 oz. fresh-squeezed grapefruit juice

½ oz. fresh-squeezed lime juice

½ oz. simple syrup

lime wheel for garnish

black cherry for garnish

Combine all ingredients in a mixing glass. Add ice and shake vigorously. Strain into a chilled cocktail glass. Garnish with a lime wheel and a black cherry on a skewer.

HOLY BANANA COW

1 oz. Shango rum

1 oz. crème de banana

1½ oz. cream

dash grenadine

banana slice for garnish

grated nutmeg for garnish

Shake with crushed ice and strain into a glass. Top with a slice of banana and sprinkle lightly with nutmeg.

HOT BUTTERED RUM

1 oz. Whaler's Vanille rum, per serving

1 cup sugar

1 cup brown sugar

1 cup butter

2 cups vanilla ice cream

¾ cup boiling water, per serving

grated nutmeg for garnish

Combine sugars and butter in a 2-quart saucepan. Cook over low heat, stirring until butter is melted. Combine cooked mixture with ice cream in large mixing bowl and beat at medium speed until smooth. Store refrigerated up to 2 weeks or frozen up to a month. For each serving, fill ¼ of a mug with mixture, and add 1 oz. Whaler's Vanille Rum and ¾ cup boiling water. Sprinkle with nutmeg.

HOT RUM AND CIDER PUNCH

1 bottle (750 ml) Don Q light rum

½ gallon apple cider

cloves for garnish

lemon slices for garnish

cinnamon sticks for garnish

Pour Don Q light rum into a bowl and add heated apple cider. Stir. Garnish with lemon slices stuck with cloves. Add a cinnamon stick to each punch cup to enhance flavor. Serves 12.

HOT VOODOO DADDY

1 oz. VooDoo spiced rum

½ oz. butterscotch schnapps

5 oz. hot chocolate

whipped cream to top

Combine first three ingredients in a mug and top with whipped cream.

HOURGLASS

1½ oz. Admiral Nelson's Premium spiced rum

4 oz. orange juice

splash grenadine

Serve over ice.

HUMMER

1 oz. Admiral Nelson's Premium spiced rum

1 oz. Caffe Lolita coffee

2 scoops vanilla ice cream

Blend with crushed ice and serve in a decorative glass.

HURRICANE ANDREW

1 oz. Cockspur Five Star colored rum

1 oz. Cockspur white rum

1 oz. orgeat syrup

1 oz. passion fruit juice

3 oz. orange juice

½ oz. lime juice

maraschino cherries for garnish

orange slice for garnish

Shake well with ice and pour into a chilled hurricane glass. Garnish with maraschino cherries, an orange slice, and an umbrella.

ICE BREAKER

½ oz. Myers's Original dark rum

¼ oz. créme de noya

¼ oz. cognac

¼ oz. gin

2 oz. lemon juice

1 oz. orange juice

Shake.

IN THE PINK

1¼ oz. Myers's Original rum cream

1 oz. Coco Lopez real cream of coconut

1 tsp. grenadine

    Blend with ice.

INDIFFERENT MISS

¾ oz. Captain Morgan Original spiced rum

¾ oz. lime juice

1 tsp. simple syrup

3 oz. club soda

Pour the rum, juice, and syrup over ice in a glass. Stir. Add the soda and stir gently.

INTERNATIONAL MAI TAI

½ oz. Malibu rum

½ oz. Myers's Original dark rum

½ oz. rum

1 tsp. orgeat syrup

2 oz. pineapple juice

2 oz. sweet and sour mix

Blend with ice. Serve in a tall glass.

ISLA GRANDE ICED TEA

1½ oz. Puerto Rican dark rum

3 oz. pineapple juice

3 oz. unsweetened brewed iced tea

lemon or lime slice for garnish

Pour into a tall glass with ice. Garnish with a lemon or lime slice.

ISLAND SUNSET

1 oz. Whaler's Rare Reserve rum

1 oz. Whaler's Great White rum

1 tbsp. passion fruit syrup

2 tsp. lime juice

dash grenadine

lime wedge for garnish

Shake and pour into a chilled hurricane glass over ice. Garnish with lime wedge.

ISLAND VOODOO

1½ oz. VooDoo spiced rum

1½ oz. RedRum

2 oz. guava juice

2 oz. mango juice

½ oz. fresh lime juice

½ oz. fresh lemon juice

Blend with ice and serve in a tall glass.

ITALIAN COLADA

1½ oz. Puerto Rican white rum

¾ oz. sweet cream

¼ oz. Coco Lopez real cream of coconut

2 oz. pineapple juice

¼ oz. amaretto

Blend with 1 scoop crushed ice.

JADE

1½ oz. Puerto Rican white rum

¾ oz. lime juice

1 tbsp. sugar

dash triple sec

dash green créme de menthe

    Shake. Serve over ice.

JAMAICA SNOW

1¼ oz. rum

½ oz. blue curaçao

2 oz. Coco Lopez real cream of coconut

2 oz. pineapple juice

    Blend with 2 cups ice.

JAMAICAN HOLIDAY

1 1/3 oz. Appleton Estate V/X Jamaica rum

½ peach (peeled or canned)

juice of ½ lime

1 tsp. sugar

peach wedge for garnish

Blend with 1 scoop crushed ice. Serve in a cocktail glass. Garnish with a peach wedge.

JAMAICAN SHAKE

1 shot Myers's Original dark rum

½ shot blended whiskey

2 oz. milk or cream

Blend with ice.

JAMAICAN SUNSET

2 oz. Wray & Nephew rum

2 oz. cranberry juice

3 oz. fresh-squeezed orange juice

Shake all ingredients with ice and strain into an ice-filled Collins glass.

JAMAICAN WAKE-UP CALL

1½ oz. Appleton Estate V/X Jamaica rum

hot black coffee to fill

whipped cream to top

    Pour Appleton Estate V/X Jamaica rum into a coffee mug. Fill with coffee and top with whipped cream.

JEALOUS LOVER

2 oz. Starr African rum

3 large strawberries

½ oz. fresh lime juice

½ oz. pineapple juice

¾ oz. simple syrup

Muddle strawberries. Shake with ice and strain into a martini glass.

JONESTOWN COOL-AID

2 oz. RedRum

½ oz. pineapple juice

½ oz. cranberry juice

Shake with ice. Serve as a cocktail or shots.

JUMBLE BREW

1 oz. Cruzan coconut rum

1 oz. Cruzan pineapple rum

3 oz. orange juice

lime squeeze

Mix first three ingredients and add a squeeze of lime. Pour into a tall glass over ice. Garnish with an exotic flower.

JUMP UP AND KISS ME

½ oz. Sea Wynde rum

½ oz. Liquore Galliano

½ oz. Marie Brizard's Apry apricot liqueur

dash Dr. Swami & Bone Daddy's gourmet sweet and sour mix

orange juice

pineapple juice

Shake first five ingredients with ice and strain into a Collins glass. Fill with orange juice and pineapple juice.

JUMP UP BANANA-NANA

1/3 cup Cruzan banana rum

1 med. banana

1 lime, squeezed

1 tbsp. honey or fine powdered sugar

1 tsp. vanilla extract

pineapple wedge for garnish

cherry for garnish

Blend with 2 cups crushed ice until smooth. Pour into a stemmed glass and garnish with a pineapple wedge and a cherry.

JUNGLE FLAME

2 oz. Starr African rum

fresh lemon wedge

¼ oz. simple syrup

lemon-lime soda

Cut up lemon and place pieces in a mixer with ice, Starr African rum, and syrup. Pour into a highball glass. Top with lemon-lime soda.

THE KAHLUA COLADA

½ oz. rum

1 oz. Coco Lopez real cream of coconut

2 oz. pineapple juice

1 oz. Kahlúa

Blend with 1 cup ice.

KEY LIME DREAM

1½ oz. light rum

¾ oz. Rose's lime juice

2 scoops vanilla ice cream

    Blend with ice.

KEY WEST SONG

1¼ oz. Captain Morgan Original spiced rum

1 oz. cream of coconut

2 oz. orange juice

Blend until smooth with 1 cup ice and pour into a glass.

KILLA' COLA

2 oz. Whaler's Killer coconut rum

½ oz. Hypnotiq

4 oz. cola

cherry for garnish

Pour into a cocktail glass over ice and garnish with a cherry.

KILLER COLADA

3 oz. Whaler's Killer coconut rum

3 tbsp. coconut milk

3 tbsp. crushed pineapples

pineapple wedge for garnish

2 cherries for garnish

Blend at high speed with 2 cups crushed ice. Pour into a chilled hurricane glass and garnish with pineapple wedge and cherries.

"KILLER" RITA

2 oz. Whaler's Killer coconut rum

1 oz. triple sec

1 oz. pineapple juice

½ oz. coconut milk

salt to rim glass

maraschino cherries for garnish

Rim a margarita glass with salt. Mix and pour into margarita glass over ice. Garnish with maraschino cherries.

KINGSTON COFFEE

4 oz. fresh-brewed coffee

1 oz. Myers's rum

dollop whipped cream

powdered bittersweet chocolate for sprinkling

cinnamon stick for garnish

Pour first two ingredients into a coffee cup or mug. Top with whipped cream and sprinkle powdered bittersweet chocolate on top. Garnish with a cinnamon stick.

KINGSTON COSMO

2 oz. Appleton Estate V/X Jamaica rum

½ oz. Cointreau

splash cranberry juice

lime squeeze

Pour first two ingredients into a glass. Top with cranberry juice and lime squeeze.

KINGSTON SOUR

1½ oz. Wray & Nephew rum

fresh pear slice (plus another for garnish)

½ oz. apple juice

½ oz. apricot brandy

dash sour mix

1/8 oz. crème de cassis

Muddle first three ingredients, then shake hard with all other ingredients over ice. Strain into an ice-filled highball glass. Garnish with a pear slice.

KOKO-COLA

1½ oz. Cruzan coconut rum

2 oz. soda

squeeze lime

Mix with ice and serve on the rocks.

KON-TIKI

1½ oz. Seven Tiki rum

2 oz. mango nectar

2 oz. cranberry juice

dash absinthe

Pour into a highball glass with ice. Stir.

LABADU

3 oz. Malibu rum

3 oz. pineapple juice

1 oz. milk or vanilla ice cream

Blend with ice.

LADY HAMILTON

1½ oz. Pusser's rum

1 tsp. fresh lime juice

Equal parts:

    passion fruit juice
    orange juice
    ginger ale

LAUGHTER

1½ oz. Cockspur Old Gold rum

1 oz. lime juice

1 tsp. sugar

3–4 mint leaves

club soda to top

Combine lime juice, mint, and sugar in a Collins or highball glass. Stir gently to bruise the mint. Fill glass ¾ with ice. Add the Cockspur Old Gold rum. Top with soda. Stir well.

LIGHT 'N STORMY

2 oz. 10 Cane rum

3–4 oz. ginger beer

½ oz. fresh-squeezed lime juice

lime wedge for garnish

candied ginger for garnish

Fill a highball glass ¾ full with ice. Combine all ingredients and stir. Garnish with lime wedge and candied ginger.

LIME FIZZ

2 oz. Brinley gold lime rum

3 oz. club soda (or lemon-lime soda if you like it sweeter)

1 lime wedge

Pour first two ingredients into a glass. Squeeze in and garnish with lime wedge.

LIME LUAU

1 oz. Whaler's Big Island banana rum

2 oz. vodka

dash lime juice

dash orange syrup

Stir with ice and serve in cocktail glass.

LIMÓN MERINGUE PIE SHOT DRINK

2 oz. Bacardi Limón rum

1 oz. Disaronno Originale amaretto

powdered sugar

ready-to-use whipped cream (preferably in a can)

Have someone sprinkle powdered sugar on your tongue, then take a drink of Bacardi Limón topped with Disaronno amaretto, but don't swallow. Have someone spray whipped cream in your mouth, then shake and swallow a little slice of pie.

LOVE POTION

1 oz. rum

½ oz. banana liqueur

½ oz. triple sec

1 oz. orange juice

1 oz. pineapple juice

orange slice for garnish

pineapple slice for garnish

banana slice for garnish

Garnish with orange, pineapple, and banana slices.

LOVE STICK

2 oz. Cockspur Five Star colored rum

1 oz. Cockspur white rum

½ oz. triple sec

1 oz. pineapple juice

1 oz. orange juice

1 oz. lime juice

¾ oz. fruit syrup

Shake well with ice. Pour into a tall glass.

LUCKY LADY

¾ oz. Bacardi light rum

¼ oz. Hiram Walker anisette

¼ oz. Hiram Walker white créme de cacao

¾ oz. cream

MALIBU ACOMPÁÑAME

2 parts Malibu coconut rum

1 part Hiram Walker triple sec

splash fresh lime juice

MALIBU AFTER TAN

1 part Malibu coconut rum

1 part white crème de cacao

2 scoops vanilla ice cream

Blend with ice and serve in a specialty glass.

MALIBU BANANA COW

1½ parts cream

1 part Malibu Tropical banana rum

1 part Malibu coconut rum

dash grenadine

grated nutmeg for sprinkling

banana slices for garnish

Shake and strain into a cocktail glass. Sprinkle with nutmeg and garnish with banana slices.

MALIBU BANANA-BERRY SPLIT

1 part Malibu Tropical banana rum

1 part Stoli Razberi vodka

lemon juice

simple syrup

Shake with ice and serve in a shot glass.

MALIBU BANANA MANGO BREEZE

1 part Malibu Tropical banana rum

1 part Malibu mango rum

1 part fresh sour mix

1 part cranberry juice

MALIBU BANANA PADDY

1 part Malibu Tropical banana rum

1 part Kahlúa

splash peppermint schnapps

MALIBU BANANA SPLIT

1 part Malibu Tropical banana rum

splash amaretto

splash crème de cacao

whipped cream for garnish

cherry for garnish

Garnish with whipped cream and a cherry.

MALIBU BANANA TROPIC-TINI

1½ parts Malibu Tropical banana rum

½ part peach schnapps

dollop mango puree

splash passion fruit nectar

cherry for garnish

Shake and serve as a martini. Garnish with a cherry.

MALIBU BANANA ZINGER

2 oz. Malibu Tropical banana rum

2 scoops lemon sherbet

2 oz. sour mix

lemon wedge for garnish

Mix in blender with 2 cups ice. Garnish with lemon wedge. Makes 2 drinks.

MALIBU BEACH

1½ oz. Malibu rum

1 oz. Smirnoff vodka

4 oz. orange juice

Serve over ice.

MALIBU BLUE LAGOON

1 part Malibu coconut rum

4 parts pineapple juice

¾ part blue curaçao

MALIBU CARIBENO

3 parts Malibu coconut rum

1 part Martel cognac

½ part pineapple

½ part fresh lemon juice

lemon wedge for garnish

Serve on the rocks. Garnish with a lemon wedge.

MALIBU COCO COLADA MARTINI

3 parts Malibu coconut rum

1 part Hiram Walker triple sec

½ part Coco Lopez real cream of coconut

½ part fresh lime juice

lime wedge for garnish

Serve in a martini glass. Garnish with lime wedge.

MALIBU COCO-COSMO

2 parts Malibu coconut rum

splash triple sec

splash pomegranate juice

splash cranberry juice

dash lime juice

lime twist for garnish

Shake with ice and strain into a martini glass. Garnish with lime twist.

MALIBU COCO-LIBRE

1 part Malibu coconut rum

3 parts cola

lime slice for garnish

Serve over ice in a tall glass. Garnish with a lime slice.

MALIBU COCONUT CREAMSICLE

2 parts Malibu coconut rum

1 scoop frozen vanilla yogurt

orange juice to fill

Pour first two ingredients into a glass and fill with orange juice. Stir. Serve as a float drink. Can also be mixed in a blender and served as a shake.

MALIBU COCONUT REFRESHER

2 parts Malibu coconut rum

2 parts lemon-lime soda

1 part lime juice

Serve over ice in a tall glass.

MALIBU ENDLESS SUMMER

2 parts Malibu Tropical banana rum

1 lemon wedge

1 lime wedge

banana slices for garnish

Crush lemons and limes. Add Malibu Tropical banana rum. Shake and strain into a martini glass. Garnish with banana slices.

MALIBU FRENCH KICK

1 part Malibu passion fruit rum

splash Martell cognac

splash lemon juice

splash simple syrup

MALIBU ISLA VIRGEN

2 parts Malibu coconut rum

½ part peach liquor

½ part amaretto

MALIBU MANGO BAY BREEZE

2 parts Malibu mango rum

1½ parts cranberry juice

1½ parts pineapple juice

MALIBU MANGO KAMIKAZE

1 part Malibu mango rum

1 part Stoli citrus vodka

½ part triple sec

¾ part fresh lime juice

MALIBU MANGO-LIME MARTINI

1½ parts Malibu mango rum

1½ parts Stoli Vanil vodka

1 part lime juice

1 part simple syrup

MALIBU MANGO MAI TAI

2 parts Malibu mango rum

1 part orange juice

1 part pineapple juice

splash lime juice

splash simple syrup

¼ oz. dark rum

Pour first five ingredients into a glass and carefully float dark rum on top.

MALIBU MARGARITA

1¼ parts Malibu coconut rum

1 part Tezon tequila

½ part blue curaçao

½ part fresh lime juice

1½ part sweetened lemon juice

Shake contents in an iced mixing glass and strain into an iced house specialty glass. Garnish with a lime wedge.

MALIBU MEGA-NUT

2 parts Malibu coconut rum

dash hazelnut liqueur

lemon-lime soda

shaved coconut flakes for garnish

Pour first two ingredients into a tall glass with ice and fill with lemon-lime soda. Garnish with shaved coconut flakes.

MALIBU MEXICANA MAMA

1 part Malibu coconut rum

½ part Kahlúa coffee liqueur

½ part white crème de menthe

1½ parts heavy cream

Shake with ice and strain into a glass over crushed ice. Garnish with 2 mint leaves.

MALIBU MIDNIGHT BREEZE

1 part Malibu coconut rum

½ part Malibu Tropical banana rum

1 part blue curaçao

pineapple juice to fill

Build with ice. Can be left shaken or layered.

MALIBU NOCHE LIBRE

1 part Malibu coconut rum

3 parts cola

splash lime juice

lime wedge for garnish

Serve in a Collins glass. Garnish with lime wedge.

MALIBU ON THE BEACH

1 oz. Malibu rum

½ oz. Baileys Irish cream

Serve as a shot.

MALIBU ORANGE COLADA

1½ oz. Malibu rum

1 oz. triple sec

4 oz. Coco Lopez real cream of coconut

MALIBU ORANGE PASSION

1 part Malibu passion fruit rum

1 part Stoli vodka

2 parts orange juice

MALIBU PASSION FRUIT COSMO

1 part Malibu passion fruit rum

1 part Stoli Vanil vodka

1 part tonic water splash cranberry juice

MALIBU PASSION FRUIT SAKE-TINI

1 part Malibu passion fruit rum

1 part Stoli vodka

½ part sake

splash passion fruit puree

MALIBU PASSION POPPER

1 part Malibu passion fruit rum

splash cola

splash cherry juice

Shake with ice and strain into a shot glass.

MALIBU PASSION TEA

1 part Malibu passion fruit rum

2 parts iced tea

1 part lemon-lime soda

lime slice for garnish

Serve over ice in a tall glass. Garnish with lime slice.

MALIBU PINEAPPLE COSMOPOLITAN

1½ parts Malibu pineapple rum

¾ part Hiram Walker triple sec

¾ part fresh lime juice

¾ part cranberry juice

lime wedge for garnish

Shake in an iced mixing glass and strain into a chilled cocktail glass. Garnish with lime wedge.

www.ingramcontent.com/pod-product-compliance
Lightning Source LLC
Chambersburg PA
CBHW071817080526
44589CB00012B/821